The Ultimate

Guide to

Successful

Job

Searching

M. L. Miller

Published by SoaringME Publishing

ISBN-13: 978-1-956874-10-5

CONTENTS

Preface

Dear Reader,

My journey to writing this book began in 1997 when I visited a recruiting firm looking for employment. The office had a wall full of awards in the lobby, over forty recruiters working in the back, and the owner Larry was full of energy and enthusiasm. Instead of finding me a job with one of their clients, Larry convinced me to work for him as a recruiter. I've been gaining knowledge about talent acquisition, recruiting, interviewing, and job searches ever since.

Over the years, I worked with well over one hundred thousand job seekers and I have seen firsthand the most effective methods of job searching and networking. In 2010, I started SoaringME to help candidates improve their job search and interviewing skills.

In this book, I outline what I've seen the most successful job searchers do to secure the most interviews for the best jobs. While it is possible to obtain a few interviews using only one or two traditional search methods, there are steps you can take that will increase your success rate, including mapping out your job search plan. The techniques and methods I put forth will help you become more competitive, prevent missed opportunities, and improve the likelihood of securing your desired job.

Best of luck, and I hope that this book helps you achieve your career goals!

M. L. Miller

Founder, SoaringME

If you enjoy this book, please post a review.

Visit

SoaringME.com

for additional resources.

Introduction

Searching for your next job can be overwhelming, but there are steps you can take to improve your chances of success. Crafting impactful resumes, using social media effectively, and tapping into the hidden job market can transform your challenging job search into securing the role of your dreams.

Imagine yourself in a scenario where you enter a restaurant looking to order your favorite meal. The waiter presents you with options: the plain version or variations with extra seasonings, ingredients, or complementary side dishes. It's likely that you, as most others do, choose a variation with extras. None of these versions will be ordered by every restaurant customer, but the variations that offer more will be preferred most often. This serves as an appropriate analogy for your job search efforts. Relying solely on traditional search methods may occasionally produce success, but incorporating additional approaches will elevate your candidacy, providing a competitive advantage and increasing your appeal in the marketplace of potential employers.

When I was initially trained as a recruiter back in 1997, I was taught that at any given time about twenty percent of the workforce is actively seeking a new job, sixty percent are passive candidates not actively looking but are open to changing jobs for the right opportunity, and the remaining twenty percent are not going to leave their job. In my experience this is fairly accurate, although depending upon economic conditions I find that in the United States it can fluctuate to be around thirty percent actively looking for a job, sixty percent passive, and ten percent not interested.

I share this to demonstrate that there is a lot of competition you'll face in your search for a job. The most attractive job opportunities usually have the most candidates contending to win the role. Not only do employers have active applicants for their open jobs, but there are also passive candidates that you'll be compared against. If you fail to utilize every search method available, you risk fading into the vast sea of candidates in the employers' mind.

However, there are techniques and tools that will give you the advantages you'll need to stand out from the crowd.

Before creating your search plan, you need to first clarify your career goals. Having a clear understanding of what you need to accomplish will lead you to be more strategic and identify which potential job opportunities align best with these goals. The most effective job seekers take the time to craft a well thought out and measurable strategy. It will also be critical for you to evaluate your progress from time to time, make necessary adjustments, and stay motivated throughout your search.

Most job seekers rely solely on methods that are familiar and comfortable, such as job postings and their small circle of friends. This provides you with an opportunity to take advantage of the approaches that they are neglecting. The key factors that you have control over are the effort you put into your job search, and the number of methods you choose to employ. You will need to decide which techniques and methods covered in this book should be part of your plan. The more strategies and tools you use, the more robust your results will be, increasing your chances of landing the job you want.

The Ideal Candidate

To achieve success in your job search, it's important to understand what potential employers are looking for in the person they want to hire. Devoting enough time up front to fully grasp what the ideal profile for your desired job looks like will increase the likelihood of you achieving your job search goals.

Companies start the hiring process with an outline of the duties that they need completed, and then develop a profile of who they think will be the best employee to do this role. Depending on the organization's size, the hiring manager, Human Resources, Talent Acquisition, upper management, or a combination of these may create this persona. The profile of the optimal hire can be influenced by the hiring manager's personal preferences, the team's current makeup, and qualities of the previous employee.

The profile of the ideal person to hire will include hard skills, soft skills, and personality traits. These characteristics will vary slightly from company to company. There are, however, some qualities that most employers are looking for in a new employee. These attributes may not even be listed in the job advertisement, but they are still things that interviewers are evaluating you on and understanding these hidden traits will give you an advantage over other candidates.

Here are the ten most common universal traits that employers are seeking.

1. Competence.

2. Passion for that work.

3. Self-motivation.

4. Works well with others.

5. Effective communication skills.

6. Ability to take responsibility for work and mistakes.

7. Good problem-solving skills.

8. Honesty.

9. Ability to listen and follow directions.

10. Reliability.

To identify the perfect candidate for a job, companies typically have a list of desired qualities and attributes, including educational background, training, experience, and personality traits. These may consist of a college degree, a specific major, certifications, industry experience, knowledge of relevant software programs or programming languages, or other tools required for that role. The personality of the ideal candidate might be that of someone who is coachable, someone who is driven and desires future advancement, a good team player, or someone who can work independently.

The interview process is a series of steps meant to evaluate how well a candidate matches this ideal person. It is even more accurate to describe the processes as being designed to eliminate the candidates who are not a good fit. The job advertisement, the questions asked during the interviews, the decision about which candidates are interviewed, and who the job offer will go to are all based on this persona.

Understanding the profile for a job is therefore critical to success, as every company has a preconceived notion of the person they want to hire. The profile is divided into two sides: the skills or experience side and the personality or compatibility with the company culture side. By having a solid grasp of these traits, you can position yourself as the best-suited candidate and increase your chances of securing an interview and eventually the job.

Here are the best steps to understanding the ideal profile for a specific job.

1.   Research 10-20 job ads for similar jobs. Make a list of the duties required and desired attributes listed in all these advertisements.

2.   Research the backgrounds of employees who are currently in similar roles. Look at 10-20 online profiles and the background they had before being hired for a job like the one you want.

3.   Ask contacts in your professional network what they think makes people successful in that job, or if they know what type of candidate that company prefers to hire for that type of role.

4.   Compile the attributes that repeatedly show up in your research. This is a great starting point for understanding what the interviewers are going to evaluate you against.

For the job you are targeting, review the list of required and desired attributes in the job ad. Companies usually list their most desired trait first, and then in descending order by level of importance. I have included a series of exercises like this one to help you understand the profile of the job that you are targeting. The *COMPANION WORKBOOK The Ultimate Guide to Successful Job Interviewing* includes exercises that can help you understand what the employer is seeking for the job you're interested in.

Most of your answers and interactions in your search should highlight the areas in your background that relate to this ideal candidate they wish to hire. Make sure not to sidetrack your interactions with a lot of irrelevant information. For example, a job ad for a nurse or therapist at a skilled nursing facility may list experience in working with elderly patients as a major component. Throughout your job search, you should highlight your experience in this area. A software engineer will often work as part of a team, so if that is your target job you should highlight and demonstrate effective communication skills.

I once worked with a candidate who was interviewing for a Vice President role with a small startup client of mine. Part of the personality profile that the Chief Executive Officer desired was somebody who is assertive and would not hesitate to advance the projects that this employee would be working on. The candidate had the education and experience for the job, therefore she initially seemed like a great match. But then she was very tentative in making her decisions and moved slowly to schedule her second interview. This gave the CEO the impression that she did not match what he was looking for on the personality side of the profile and she was removed from consideration. Had she understood the profile more fully, perhaps that would have changed her behavior, but it's likely she simply wasn't the right fit to begin with. It's crucial to note that comprehending the optimal profile does not imply that you should pretend to be someone else, but rather showcase how you meet the requirements through your conduct and responses during the job search and interview process.

Employers' Sources of New Hires

One of the most effective ways to find your new job is to make yourself more discoverable for those who are searching for the right candidate. Understanding where recruiters and hiring managers typically find their new hires will help you become more visible in their search efforts. Employers track the data for recruitment sources of new hires to show them which recruiting efforts are most worth their time and money. When a new hire starts with an organization, the talent acquisition or human resources team creates a report to track the initial recruiting source of that candidate. This data will be part of calculating the Return on Investment (ROI) of the employers' recruiting budget. In advanced organizations they track the employees' duration of employment, performance reviews, and promotions to link a Quality of Hire (QoH) metric to each recruiting source of candidates.

There are various sources from which employers find new employees to hire. The significance of each source of new talent depends on the industry and level of position. Employers use a combination of these sources to find the right candidates to hire. I will provide additional details on how you can best maneuver within these sources in later chapters, but it will benefit your job search to understand where the employers are looking for their candidates.

Typical Employer Sources of Hires:

- Employee Referrals.
- Network Referrals.
- Internal Candidates.
- Former Employees.
- Outside Recruiting Agencies.
- Job Advertisements (company website, job boards).
- Directly Sourced by the Employers' Talent Acquisition Department (social media/communication tools/sourcing software).
- Job Fairs (in-person/online events).
- Career Centers.
- Conversion of Contingent Staff.

- Conversion of Interns.
- Military Recruitment Programs.
- Soft Recruiting Events.

Employee Referrals.

Just as it sounds, an employee referral is a job candidate that is referred to the hiring team by one of the current employees at the company. As a company grows and becomes more established, they typically will create a formal program which financially rewards employees for referring a candidate who ends up getting hired.

I have seen studies that show employee referrals make up anywhere from 10% to as much as 50% of new hires depending on the industry. From my experience, and conversations with others in talent acquisition and human resources I believe that the range is most commonly between 5% and 25%.

I've heard some claim incorrectly that employee referrals make up the largest source of new hires. This is not usually the case, but for most employers they are the greatest source of quality hires.

By quality I mean that a larger percentage of these employees do well in the job, compared to candidates from other sources. Because of this, companies tend to make an extra effort to interview these referrals. There are some new services that you can pay for, who then offer money to employees of companies to get them to refer you. This may work in some instances, but employers are aware of these services and these types of referrals will end up generating additional scrutiny for the employee and the candidate. I cannot recommend that you use any of these services, you will be better served by building your own network and getting referred using the direct route.

Network Referrals.

A network referral is a candidate that is referred by a former colleague, professional associate, or family friend of the employers' current employees. These candidates also are viewed in high regard by most employers, and most likely will be interviewed.

Internal Candidates.

For your job search, internal candidates do create more competition, but it is usually a very good sign when an employer regularly considers its own employees who want a promotion.

Former Employees.

Former employees who left under good circumstances are another source of competition for you in your job search, and a good sign of an employer when former employees are willing to return. Many large employers maintain closed alumni social media or communication platforms to keep in contact with former employees. Your former employers may also be worth exploring as part of your job search.

Outside Recruiting Agencies.

Third-Party or outside recruiters typically specialize in their recruiting efforts to focus on a specific geography, type of job, industry, level of role, or a combination of these factors. Outside recruiters build relationships with employers within their area of specialization. They can be a very valuable resource for you in your job search, as they often have a direct line of communication to the hiring managers and/or corporate recruiters with whom they can advocate for you to be interviewed and eventually hired.

Job Advertisements (company website, job boards).

These ads will almost always be posted on the careers/employment page of the corporate website, and then also on one or more third-party job boards.

Job ads are typically the largest source of candidates and new hires for most employers. You are likely familiar with the largest job boards and the niche sites within your industry.

Directly Sourced by the Employers' Talent Acquisition Department (social media/communication tools/sourcing software).

Up until the 2005-2015 period, almost all corporate recruiting teams would rely on outside firms for the proactive recruiting on their open jobs. These days, many talent acquisition departments search online for viable candidate profiles on social media, communication tools or through specialized recruiting software. The best thing for you to know is how to make yourself visible, or "locatable" to these recruiters when they are searching. I'll cover more on this later.

Job Fairs (in-person/online events).

You are likely already familiar with job fairs. Recently, many companies have begun offering online versions.

Career Centers.

You can find career centers at colleges/universities, local government employment centers, some non-profit organizations, and occasionally a private business.

Conversion of Contingent Staff.

Temporary workers, contractors, corp-2-corp, and freelancers are basically hired as non-permanent employees. But, as the hiring manager and co-workers get to know the quality of the work they receive from these temporary employees, they often decide to offer them a permanent role.

Conversion of Interns.

An internship is another type of temporary worker. Usually, interns are current students at a university but can also be part of some other job development program. An internship program provides the employer with a pool of potential candidates for permanent jobs.

Military Recruitment Programs.

Employers often partner with military focused recruitment agencies, attend ex/transitioning military job fairs, and build relationships with military groups and organizations. Typically, employers recruit ex-military candidates for jobs that directly relate to their military specialty, or because they have the makings of a good leader if trained properly.

Soft Recruiting Events.

These events are designed to be relaxed social gatherings where job seekers can interact with hiring managers, recruiters, and employees to gain insight into the employers' culture. This approach allows the organization to learn more about the job candidate's personality and potential fit within the company.

These events may be organized by the employer, a recruiter, an association, or even a university. Many industries, particularly technology, financial services, and healthcare, use these types of events to source potential new hires.

Now that you have an overview of where employers look for their job candidates, in the following chapters I will explain how you can best use these sources to get yourself more of the interviews that you want.

Aligning with the Ideal Profile

Having discussed what employers want to hire and where they find job candidates, now we explore effective ways that you can utilize this information. Recruiters regularly search online profiles to find potential candidates that they wish to contact about an open job. Hiring managers and recruiters also review online profiles of job applicants. Inconsistencies between your profiles, resume, and how you present yourself will create unnecessary doubt about your suitability for the job. You need to consider what your desired employers are seeking to hire, and then consistently demonstrate the ways that you match that profile.

Unique Value Proposition (UVP).

Your UVP is a distinctive and compelling statement that communicates the specific benefits and advantages your employment offers which sets you apart from your competitors. Essentially, your UVP answers the crucial question: "Why should I hire you over others?". It should be concise, specific, persuasive and should capture the attention and interest of potential employers, ultimately influencing them to want to hire you. Crafting a strong UVP is vital for a successful job search in a competitive market.

The strategic process to create your unique value proposition starts by thoroughly understanding the ideal candidate profile for your target jobs. Next, focus on highlighting your skills, experience, education, or attributes that overlap with this preferred profile and sets you apart from most of the other candidates. Emphasize the professional strengths, accomplishments, and the specific value that you bring to an employer and how it addresses the challenges they face. Your UVP should only be two or maybe three sentences long, and it should sound natural and sincere.

Stay away from hyperbole and whenever possible use quantifiable metrics to demonstrate the impact of your past contributions. This could include a unique blend of technical expertise, soft skills, and industry-specific knowledge. Consider your professional achievements, such as successful projects, measurable results, or innovations, and highlight these. Craft a clear and concise statement that is focused on the employers, addressing the "what's in it for them" question.

Be sure that your value proposition is both memorable and easily understood. Use simple language and avoid industry jargon. You should test your UVP with a small sample of your target audience to gather feedback and then refine it accordingly. Finally, you need to integrate your UVP consistently across your resume, cover letter, all your online channels, and your elevator pitch to reinforce your unique value in the minds of potential employers. Regularly revisit and update your value proposition as needed to stay competitive in your job search.

UVP for a candidate seeking their first management role.

"I've demonstrated my ability to motivate and guide teams to success in my current role as a team leader. By spearheading the implementation of new streamlined processes, I achieved a 20% increase in productivity within six months. I will be able to drive these types of improvements if hired for this role."

UVP for a new graduate seeking their first marketing role.

"As a recent graduate, I've honed my skills through hands-on projects, leading to a 30% increase in online engagement for a local business during an internship. I'm eager to bring my proficiency in market analysis and digital strategies to help drive measurable success for your team."

Both example value propositions will likely be very effective if they match the desired skills for the jobs being targeted.

Mistakes to avoid with your Unique Value Proposition.

When constructing your UVP do not use generic, vague statements as they will result in your value proposition blending into the background. If you overemphasize your technical skills, use lengthy jargon-laden statements, or overlook employer needs, your UVP will not resonate. If you ignore your personal branding and have inconsistency between your online presence, resume, cover letter, and the UVP, your image will be fragmented and weaken your candidacy.

Personal Candidate Brand.

While the UVP is a targeted statement emphasizing the specific value you bring to a job, a personal brand is a more comprehensive and broader image that encompasses multiple aspects of your professional identity. Building your personal candidate brand is very much like the strategy that top companies use for their products. Instead of Coca-Cola, McDonalds, or Apple emphasizing what unique qualities their company and products provide to customers, top candidates create their personal brand to emphasize the unique skills and value that they provide to employers. In lieu of corporate logos, product packaging, websites, taglines, and advertising campaigns, a personal candidate brand uses social media profiles, professional headshots, resume/CV, cover letter, portfolio of work, email signature, personal website, recommendation letters, and certifications/work assessments to emphasize a distinct and positive image to differentiate you from other candidates.

In tight job markets competition can be intense, making it difficult for you to stand out. One of the most effective ways to distinguish yourself in the job market is to develop a strong personal candidate brand. When most people think of major company brands, they immediately know what products or services that company provides, and usually have an impression about the level of quality or value. A personal candidate brand can do the same thing for you with recruiters and hiring managers.

There is well known phrase that I believe began in the public relations industry, "perception is reality". A well-done brand can create the perception with employers that you are the strongest match to the profile they are seeking. Your candidate brand is a unique and compelling representation of your professional identity, skills, value, and experience. The best job seekers establish a clear identity, communicate their value proposition to potential employers, and stand out from the competition.

Clarifying your professional identity and value proposition can help you to build credibility and trust with potential employers. By presenting a clear and consistent image, you can strengthen how they perceive you as a candidate.

A personal candidate brand based on tangible skills, education and experience is much more persuasive than one based on puffery. I have conducted recruitment searches where I came across candidate profiles that were filled with subjective descriptive words. These profiles that rely heavily on words such as "Hard Working", "Dynamic", "Motivated", "Exceptional", "Thought Leader", or similar words are unpersuasive and less effective than profiles that focus on tangible evidence.

Having a strong and visible personal candidate brand will make you stand out to recruiters who are looking for someone with a profile that matches the job they're trying to fill. By consistently, clearly, and authentically presenting your brand and value proposition throughout your job search, you can also overcome potential objections or concerns that employers may otherwise have. This means that if you have a potent brand, you are more likely to grab the attention of recruiters, leading to more interviews and ultimately, more job offers.

To create your personal candidate brand, start with a list of roles that might be your dream job. Then, list five roles that either feed into or build the skills necessary for your dream job. Include the industry and level of the role.

Take an honest look at your education, work history, and achievements to determine what sets you apart from most other candidates. Start with the areas where your profile overlaps with the ideal profiles of your target roles, and then the ones that feed into or build the skills for those roles. Be as specific as possible with your skills and experience.

Next, build a strong presence on social media that reflects your candidate identity. Your online presence across all platforms should include your UVP, and a professional looking headshot. Your resume and cover letter also need to be consistent with your personal candidate brand.

If the jobs you are targeting typically expect you to present your portfolio of work during the interview process, align the portfolio with your value proposition and overall candidate brand. On the personal email that you use to correspond with recruiters and hiring managers, create an email signature that conforms with this brand. Build the same consistency into any personal website, or recommendation letters that you might use throughout an interview process. If your target job requires any certifications or education, be proactive and at least begin the process of obtaining these requirements. If the certification or education is in process, include this in your candidate branding.

It is worth investing your time and effort into building your personal candidate brand, as it can make a significant difference in a competitive job search. Making connections at industry events, job fairs, and other professional social opportunities will also be part of the overall creation of your candidate brand.

To create a strong personal candidate brand.
- Identify your desired role.
- Assess your skills and experiences.
- Define your unique value proposition (UVP).

- Develop your online presence.

- Craft compelling resumes and cover letters.

- Align other relevant material with your brand. (i.e. portfolio of work, recommendation letters, email signature, etc.).

- Embed your UVP and brand into professional conversations.

- Be proactive and consistent.

- Target job opportunities that align with your brand.

Mistakes to avoid with your Candidate Brand.

Being consistent is paramount; any discrepancies across your online platforms, resumes, cover letters, and personal pitches can not only be confusing for employers, but it will make them doubt your authenticity. Ignoring feedback, overlooking soft skills, overhyping your qualifications, and not preparing adequately for interviews are common errors that you should avoid when establishing your candidate brand. Don't assume that the recruiter or hiring manager understands details about your background and how your skills and experience match with the optimal profile. You understand your background far more than we ever will, so make it obvious and clear how your experience and skills relate to the profile of the perfect fit for the job.

Resumes and Cover Letters.

The imagined ideal candidate is used to create the job description, job advertisement, interview questions, and to choose which resumes are selected for interviews. To write a successful resume, you need to tailor it to this profile. Resumes and cover letters should also be consistent with your personal candidate brand and unique value proposition.

The employers' goal is not to simply assess whether you could do the job or learn it, but rather to evaluate which applicants align best with the ideal candidate profile. It is not uncommon for certain job openings to attract a high volume of applications, sometimes several hundred, which reduces the recruiter's flexibility in making exceptions for candidates who do not fit the profile precisely. Conversely, when there are few applicants, the recruiter might be more inclined to consider candidates whose profile differs somewhat from the ideal.

Most recruiters and hiring managers have limited time to read through hundreds of resumes. The average time spent reviewing a resume is only about six seconds. In that brief time, we quickly search for keywords and phrases that align with the ideal profile. If those minimum requirements are met, we will read further to determine if there is enough overlap with the profile to warrant an interview.

Many employers use an Applicant Tracking System (ATS) software such as Lever, Greenhouse, Workday, Jobvite, SmartRecruiters, Workable, Taleo, and others to process job applications and store resumes. Some of these systems include a resume scoring service as an optional feature that employers can choose to utilize or not. The resume scoring service is designed to automatically filter and rank resumes based on how well they match specific job requirements and criteria. The system analyzes resumes and assigns a score based on keywords, work experience, education, and other factors.

Employers set up these filters by creating a list of keywords and phrases relevant to the job position they are hiring for. The ATS software then scans resumes and ranks them according to how closely they match the predefined criteria.

I have seen some online advice from inexperienced people who exaggerate the use of this feature. Stay away from anyone who tries to sell you a resume format that they claim will beat the ATS and get you an interview, it's not true at all. The ATS software systems are flawed, they often assign a score to a resume that the recruiter disagrees with, and most employers do not currently use this feature. However, advancements in artificial intelligence (AI) technology are rapidly improving the accuracy of these tools. As a result, more employers may choose to utilize this feature in the future to help streamline their recruitment process.

Recently, there has been a trend of adding colorful graphics, charts, and timelines onto resumes to stand out when conveying certain skills and experience. I do not recommend this approach as these often import incorrectly into the ATS and make it more difficult for recruiters to find the specific items they are looking for. Instead, the most effective resumes show the skills and experience the employer is seeking in a way that is easy for them to find quickly. These keywords and phrases are used in the job advertisement, which is why it is so important to tailor your resume for each job.

Your resume should be customized for every job you apply to, but also be in alignment with your personal candidate brand and UVP. While there is no solid rule on the number of pages a resume should be, it is important to remember that the person reading it will want to see what they're looking for in the first few seconds. Generally, one or two pages will be sufficient, depending on the amount of experience you have.

In some lines of work and countries outside the United States, it is common to use a Curriculum Vitae (CV) rather than a resume. The main differences are the length and the amount of detail provided. A CV is usually longer than a resume because it includes more details on academic publications, education, awards, presentations, etc. If you work in a field where a CV is common, recruiters and hiring managers will expect to see those additional details, including a list of your publications.

Cover letters are not always read, and some applications won't even accept one. While not all recruiters or hiring managers read cover letters, many do, so you should be prepared to submit one. A strong cover letter should be brief and clarify any potential gaps or questions that the reader may have after reviewing your resume. This could include explaining your motivation for wanting to change to a different company or industry, addressing short stints at previous employers, or previous gaps in employment.

Your cover letter should be one page and provide enough information to help persuade the reader that you are worth interviewing.

Mistakes to avoid with your resumes and cover letters.

Failure to align with your personal brand and value proposition can create doubt about your profile and lead to rejection. Failing to tailor your resume to that specific profile is all too common of a mistake. You should customize each application with specific keywords, phrases, skills, and experiences that match the ideal profile for that job, minimizing generic content. To use the analogy of dating, imagine coming across a person who gives the impression that they'll date anyone who shows interest in them. Candidates who don't customize their resume often come across in a similar way, they just want any job and are not especially dedicated to or a good match for that specific job.

Avoid graphics, excessive details, and listing generic common skills as they will likely distract the reader from the important attributes that make you stand out. Unnecessary information like "References available upon request" or a full address can also clutter your resume.

Do not assume that the reader of your resume will have comprehensive knowledge of the products you dealt with at previous employers. A lack of quantifiable results on your resume diminishes your credibility compared to other candidates. Including false information is the fastest way to have yourself excluded from ever being considered for any job opportunities at that employer.

Do not send 5-10 pages of additional documents with your application, we do not have time to read through reference letters, certifications, etc. Send these items once you've moved two or three steps into the interview process. Heavy use of subjective self-assessed personality traits can also be counterproductive. Even small mistakes, like grammatical errors, can leave a negative impression, so be sure to thoroughly proofread.

Social Media.

Making yourself discoverable and easily accessible to recruiters can be a game-changer for your job search. Recruiters often search social media and utilize AI-powered tools to search for qualified candidates across various platforms. By optimizing your social media presence with your skills, experience, and career goals that match the profile for your desired job, you can capture the attention of potential employers and headhunters. While social media can help to expose you to potential job opportunities, it should only complement your other job search efforts.

LinkedIn is the most well-known platform for professional networking, with over 700 million users globally. However, it is not without significant flaws, such as overpriced services and low customer service ratings. I do not recommend paying for any extra services from LinkedIn. It is also important that you establish a strong presence on multiple platforms to create your personal candidate brand.

For example, visual-based platforms such as Instagram and TikTok can be more beneficial if your career is in a creative industry. Meanwhile, specialized online communities or forums can be valuable for making connections in a particular niche or field. Regardless of which platforms you utilize, make sure that your personal candidate brand and UVP are reflected across all your presence online. By taking a proactive and deliberate approach to your social media, you can significantly improve your job search results and open new opportunities for yourself.

Fortunately for me, I was trained in locating candidates before social media existed, but most recruiters today only know how to find you through your social media profiles. I've had discussions with other recruiters about this topic and finding prospective candidates through social media is the only proactive method that most of them know. This means that if you do not make yourself available on social media, you are excluding yourself from many job opportunities.

Mistakes to avoid with your social media.

There have been multiple surveys of employers that show most of them use social media to help screen potential hires, and most have chosen to not hire at least one candidate based on their online profiles. You will jeopardize your job search by maintaining unprofessional social media accounts. If you share excessive personal information, adult language/pictures, or post aggressive, rude, or heated debate content on your social media, it will be viewed as a red flag by potential employers. Complaining about your current or past employers on social media will likely cause potential new employers to perceive you as a potential risk that is not worth their efforts to pursue.

Neglecting to highlight skills and experience on social media weakens your candidate brand and diminishes opportunities to connect with recruiters seeking specific profiles. Inconsistency in branding across your social media platforms might confuse employers and recruiters, hurting your credibility. You need to maintain a cohesive and professional image by ensuring consistency in messaging, tone, and your professional profile pictures. Ignoring social media all together or failing to actively participate means missing out on potential new job opportunities.

Communication Tools.

While social media is a powerful tool to make yourself visible and accessible to recruiters, communication platforms can also be useful for your job search. By joining industry-related groups, servers, or industry-specific teams, recruiters can discover your profile and identify you as a strong candidate. These platforms provide you with an opportunity to connect with potential employers and headhunters, plus offer a range of benefits that can help you stand out in a crowded job market.

By using these platforms, you can demonstrate your ability to communicate clearly and concisely. You can also use these platforms to ask questions and gather information about potential job opportunities, which will give you a better understanding of what the employer is looking for, so you can customize your application materials accordingly.

Several platforms have groups or channels dedicated to specific industries or job functions, making it easy to connect with other professionals in your field. Engaging in these communities can give you early insight into new job openings, industry trends, and help you to establish valuable relationships with other professionals.

When selecting which platforms to use for your job search, it's important to consider that each platform has its own set of strengths and weaknesses. Slack is an excellent choice for remote teams, while Discord is popular among gaming and creative communities. Microsoft Teams is a great option for large corporate communication and collaboration. WhatsApp is commonly used for messaging and communication with international contacts, while Skype is popular for video conferencing. Telegram offers a secure and private messaging platform, and WeChat is widely used in China. Finally, LINE is a popular communication app in Japan and other Asian countries such as Thailand.

Mistakes to avoid on your communication tools.

Choosing groups or channels for communication that are mismatched to your career goals will lead to wasted time, confusion, and even coming across as unprofessional. Ignoring platform etiquette, such as sending unsolicited messages or using rude language will give a bad impression of your professionalism, hurting your candidate brand.

Elevator Pitch.

An elevator pitch is a concise and compelling presentation that showcases your skills and acts as an introduction to perspective employers. The term generally refers to a speech of 30 seconds to two minutes long that represents a scenario where individuals find themselves in an elevator with a decision maker or someone important. The scenario depicts a brief opportunity to make a persuasive pitch in the time it takes to ride an elevator together.

It's better for you to imagine being introduced to the hiring manager or recruiter for your dream job, or to someone who can introduce you to those decision makers. This would be a brief opportunity to present your personal candidate brand and value proposition to demonstrate what a strong match you are for the job you're seeking. Think of how they will later need to explain your candidate profile to others. Your goal is to get them to explain that you are a match for what they're looking for. If you provide irrelevant information or leave relevant information out, then you will likely fail at that goal.

Your pitch can be used effectively at job fairs, networking events, in email messages, chance meetings, and interviews. You should stay far away from using a canned, memorized verbatim pitch as it will come across as very disingenuous. Stick to memorizing bullet points of your main ideas and speaking naturally when delivering your pitch. It is essential that your elevator pitch, online presence, and resume all complement one another to create a cohesive brand.

There are various approaches to crafting a powerful elevator pitch, and the right method will depend on your situation.

Problem-Solution.

This method involves identifying a problem that the employer is facing and then presenting yourself as the solution to that problem. To do this, you need to research the company and the role you're applying for, understand the challenges and pain points that the employer is experiencing, and then use an explanation of your experience and skills to position yourself as the solution to those challenges. By using this method, you can create a compelling elevator pitch that quickly captures the attention of the employer and highlights your UVP. This approach will likely differentiate you from other candidates and demonstrate how you would contribute to the success of the company. The problem-solution method helps you to focus your elevator pitch on the employer's needs and priorities, rather than just talking about yourself, and this will increase your success rate.

Personal Branding.

This method involves identifying and highlighting your unique skills, values, and strengths that align with the job and the employer's needs. To do this, you need to understand the ideal candidate profile and your personal brand. Then you can craft an elevator pitch that showcases your UVP and demonstrates how you fit the job and can add value to the company. You can create an impactful pitch that differentiates yourself from other candidates and position yourself as a strong match for the role.

Past-Present-Future.

This method involves outlining your past experiences and accomplishments, describing your current situation and expertise, and explaining your future goals and how they align with the company's mission and vision. By highlighting your past achievements, you can demonstrate your qualifications and any expertise in your field. Then, by describing your current situation and expertise, you can showcase your unique value proposition. By discussing your future goals that align with the company's vision, you can demonstrate your commitment and enthusiasm to contribute to the company's success. This method allows you to provide an engaging overview of your skills, experience, and career aspirations in a concise and impactful way.

Success Story Method.

This method for creating an elevator pitch is one that I like to compare to answering a behavioral-based interview question. It involves telling a compelling success story that showcases your skills and achievements. The story should be concise, memorable, and relatable, and it should highlight your UVP. To begin, you'll need to identify a specific problem or challenge that you faced in a previous job or project. Next, describe how you overcame the obstacle and what specific actions you took to achieve success. Finally, outline the successful results of your actions and explain how this experience has prepared you for the job you're currently seeking. Make sure that your success story relates directly to the challenges you will likely face in the job you are targeting. Think of this pitch as preemptively answering the behavioral-based interview question *"Tell me about a time when you faced ___."* (Fill in the blank with a problem or challenge that directly relates to the job you're seeking).

Quick Pitch Method.

This method revolves around a concise and strategic presentation of your professional background, skills, and aspirations. The pitch includes your value proposition, highlighting distinctive skills that align with the job and what makes you unique. You share one or two key achievements from your professional background, emphasizing measurable results. Then you connect these accomplishments to the requirements of the target role. Express genuine passion and enthusiasm for the industry and the specific role you are pursuing. Briefly outline your career goals, emphasizing how they align with the employer's vision. Conclude your pitch with a clear call to action, inviting further discussion or interviews and expressing your interest in exploring how your skills and experiences can contribute to the success of the team or company.

Mistakes to avoid with your Elevator Pitch.

A generic pitch will fail to distinguish you from other candidates and result in you being forgotten. Lengthy pitches on the other hand risk losing the listener's attention. Being completely self-centered in your focus will not convey any potential value for the employer. Using too much industry jargon or technical terms can alienate some, and a lack of enthusiasm will make your pitch fall flat. Failure to practice adequately can lead to stumbling, coming across as inauthentic. If you omit crucial details, fail to adapt to the audience, are overly aggressive, dwell excessively on the past, or neglect to ask for a clear call to action, you will undermine the effectiveness of your pitch. Do not forget to include a call to action at the end of your pitch, try to move forward in their process.

The Hidden Job Market

The hidden job market is the name for job opportunities that are not publicly advertised, posted on job boards or company websites. By developing your personal candidate brand, UVP, creating your elevator pitch, networking, working with recruiters, attending recruiting events, and sending targeted messages, you can increase your access to these hidden jobs.

There are some who wildly exaggerate the significance of the hidden job market, but the truth is that incorporating it into your overall job search plan will have a substantial impact on your likelihood of success. There are estimates claiming that up to eighty five percent of all jobs are filled through networking and existing relationships without ever being advertised. From my experience, I believe that it is somewhere between forty to sixty percent of all jobs. Even if the number is less than that, you should not be willing to miss out on any jobs simply because you're only used to applying for advertised positions. Most job seekers use job boards as their primary method of searching for new opportunities, so tapping into the hidden job market will give you a distinct competitive advantage.

Many hiring managers in a new role reach out directly to their own network to fill jobs on their new team. There are also hires that happen because the manager had been planning to add a new position and already know the candidate who they believe is the perfect fit. Occasionally, a manager meets a fantastic candidate who they see as so high value that they'll find a way to make them part of their organization, even if they need to create a new job to do it.

Hidden jobs that I have recruited for in my career include confidential searches, newly created jobs, and brief job postings that are quickly filled by someone with existing connections. Confidential recruiting searches usually involve selecting a replacement hire before the employee being replaced is aware, or recruiting for a role that the company does not want their competitors to be aware of until the last minute. Most often these searches are contracted to an outside recruitment or headhunting agency.

By tapping into these opportunities, you can potentially bypass the crowded and competitive public job market and find openings that other candidates are oblivious to. Accessing these hidden career opportunities though will require more effort and networking on your part. You will need to build relationships with people in your industry and be proactive in seeking out opportunities that are not immediately visible.

It is a mistake to think of the hidden job market as something that is exclusive to executive candidates because it also includes early career opportunities. Establishing yourself as an ideal fit for your dream job prior to the beginning of the interview process, or at the very outset, can position you as the clear frontrunner in the mind of the hiring manager. There have been numerous times in my career when I have managed an interview process like this, and a different candidate being offered the job would have required an unexpected miracle. Once a hiring manager has decided that a candidate is what they're looking for, it can be extremely difficult to change their perception.

Understanding the employer's desired candidate profile allows you to build a strong value proposition and personal candidate brand which you align throughout your resumes, cover letters, online profiles, and elevator pitch. Then you will be able to deepen your candidate brand as you speak with your professional network, recruiters, and headhunters. These are the keys to unlocking the hidden job market, but it's crucial to self-assess and adjust as you continue throughout your search.

With the right approach and persistence, the hidden job market can make a determining impact in your job search. By utilizing the tools and strategies outlined in this book, you can increase your chances of tapping into this market.

Mistakes to avoid in the hidden job market.

The most common mistake made in the hidden job market is simply failing to actively participate in it. By disregarding former colleagues, and underutilizing tools to network, you will miss out on job opportunities. If you solely rely on online applications or fail to do your research on employers, you'll lessen your chances at receiving interviews and consequently job offers. Being too passive and lacking a clear career direction are also all too common.

Networking.

The most powerful tool that you can use for a successful job search is professional networking. There are a variety of reasons why some job seekers choose not to network, but talking to people and creating connections with others in your industry will give you a significant advantage in your search. Sending messages, attending industry events, job fairs, and other social opportunities can provide excellent avenues to build your personal brand and grow your network. While it's crucial to share your unique value proposition, it's equally important for you to offer value to others as part of your networking. Candidates who are willing to offer help are much more likely to succeed in forming strong relationships that yield results.

Your networking efforts can lead to key introductions or even recommendations, insights on new job openings, as well as inside information about the people making hiring decisions. Having strong relationships with employees of one of your target employers can also create a "pull-through" effect on your job application, greatly increasing the odds that you receive an interview. Keep in mind that building relationships with people will not provide you with a benefit every time, and it will take a while to see results. However, if just a few of your contacts reciprocate, then your efforts will add an enormous amount of value to your job search. These connections can open new avenues for you and lead to job opportunities that you otherwise will not have.

Networking can also involve building connections with people outside of your industry. For example, your friends, family members, or former colleagues may have connections or know someone who can help you in your job search. This is also true for alumni of your school, former employees of the same companies as you, fraternal or social organizations, or any shared experience that you have with others. People are often willing to assist those who share a connection like this, even when their experiences were separated by decades.

Most networking conversations in your job search will begin with a message or email. Mostly these should be messages that you send, and occasionally ones that you receive because of a referral, one of your posts on social media, or just your online profile. The most successful job search networkers take a strategic approach with their messages by first creating a target list, identifying hiring managers, recruiters, and others before engaging with them.

To create your target list, start with your existing professional network. Create an initial list of your target employers, which you can continue to add to later. Search LinkedIn and other social media to see who you are already connected to that you want to include in your networking. Build on this with any industry related contacts that you have a shared experience with. Next, identify the key players in your industry and especially those at your target employers. This should include potential hiring managers, recruiters, and anyone in your network who might be able to introduce you to those key players. Sometimes a job advertisement will list the title of the hiring manager, and you can simply do an online search for that company and title.

LinkedIn does have a few features that you should take advantage of. In the main search bar, you can search for your industry or job field and add the words "I'm hiring", which is a feature that hiring managers and recruiters use on the platform. It is best to include the quotation marks around I'm hiring, and when it returns results, click on the button at the top of the page marked "people". This should produce a list of key personnel that are actively hiring in your field. You should also review the company page of your target employers and click the link for their employees. At the top of the results page, you can filter the list of people by selecting 1st and 2nd degree connections from the dropdown menu. These results are a list of employees at that target employer who are already connected to you or one of your contacts who can introduce you to them.

If you have a handful of professional contacts that will recommend you if asked, go to their LinkedIn profile to find connections that they have at your target employers. On their profile page, click on the link to their connections or your mutual connections. At the top of the results page, click on the "all filters" button. That should show you an options screen, the "connections of" your contact will be already selected. Go to the "current company" option, enter your target employers, and click on the "show results" button. This will show you any connections of your contact that work at the company you are targeting.

Connect with alumni and industry associations, or even the local Chamber of Commerce. Keep a record of the names of contacts you meet at any professional event you attend.

Years ago, there was a popular party game called "Six Degrees of Kevin Bacon". The idea was that virtually any actor can be linked to the actor Kevin Bacon within six steps or fewer. Players took turns naming any random well-known actor and tried to connect that actor to Kevin Bacon through other actors who they had worked with in a movie. Each connection represents one degree of separation. The ultimate challenge was to find the shortest path of movie connections between the chosen actor and Kevin Bacon.

This game demonstrated how we live in a small world where individuals are interconnected. It is a great analogy for how you should approach your professional networking in your job search. Think of the decision makers at your target employers like Kevin Bacon in the game and try to find the shortest path of connections between you and them. You may need to build a networking relationship with someone who is two degrees away from the decision maker, then one degree away to then finally make an effective connection with the right person.

Typical Sources to Build a Networking Target List.

- Former bosses and mentors.
- Former co-workers.
- Industry colleagues.
- Existing social media connections.
- Your second-degree connections (Contacts of your contacts).
- Desired connections at your target employers.
- Second-degree connections to your targets.
- Past customer or indirect industry contacts.
- Outside recruiters who specialize in target niche.
- Inside recruiters at your target employers.
- Inside recruiters listed on current advertised jobs.
- Hiring managers at your target employers.
- Hiring managers listed on current advertised jobs.
- Friends and family with relevant network connections.
- Contacts made at professional networking events.

- Your alumni association.

- Past professors.

- Former employees of the same companies as you.

- Industry contacts with a shared fraternal, sorority, charitable or social organization.

- Industry contacts with shared athletic or arts participation.

- Contacts from career fairs and soft recruiting events.

- Industry or job-related social media groups.

- Local business associations.

- Chambers of commerce.

- Industry contacts at volunteer organizations.

- Contacts from trade shows.

- Professional certification program contacts.

- Contacts from book clubs.

- Online forums or discussion groups.

After you've identified contacts that you wish to message, it's important to track your networking efforts. This will keep you organized on who you have or have not reached out to, and it will keep you accountable for your weekly efforts. The first couple of weeks of networking you should focus on the quantity of your activity to get used to making the effort of contacting and speaking with your network. In weeks three and four, focus on the results you're receiving such as obtaining meetings, events, or interviews. After your first month, begin to evaluate the quality of your results, such as the conversion rates of your efforts. Finally, reassess and adjust your strategy, value

 proposition, elevator pitch, or tactics as needed.

I do not recommend paying LinkedIn any extra fees, including for the feature of sending direct messages. You are better off trying to get referred through one of your existing contacts or simply sending them a connection request with an added note which includes your UVP. Recruiters are much more likely to accept these requests than hiring managers, but both will be worth your effort.

It's true that most of your networking efforts will not pay off, but it truly only takes one job offer to make it all worthwhile. The most successful job seekers maintain their focus on the aspects that they have control over. You should approach your networking efforts with the mindset that you have control of your actions, and eventually a portion of those will yield results for you.

Mistakes to avoid when networking.

Don't let yourself become intimidated and fail to network altogether, this is a critical mistake that will keep you from job opportunities. One of the other large errors I've seen is when a candidate expects help, or they feel entitled to it. If you act entitled to somebody's time or assistance in your networking, there are very few who will assist you. Ask for help and accept that some will give it, and some won't. Exhibiting excessively aggressive or assumptive behavior such as unannounced in-person visits or any inappropriate attempt to pressure someone to network with you, will do much more harm than good. Targeting the wrong individuals for networking or neglecting to follow-up afterwards will also lessen your results. Failing to offer value to your contacts, not listening, and lacking preparation for networking events are all big mistakes that you should avoid. Coming across as inauthentic will damage your professional reputation and undermine the connections you make. You should also stay away from using guerilla marketing or overly unconventional tactics in your networking efforts unless those skills relate specifically to the desired profile of your target jobs.

Recruiters and Headhunters.

Most hiring processes will involve working with a recruiter at some point, but they can also be a pivotal contributor to you obtaining more interviews. The titles of Recruiter, Headhunter, and Talent Acquisition seem to be indistinct terms to many people, but there are various categories of recruiting professionals. It will help your job search if you understand some of the distinctions, so I'll describe the primary categories. Regardless of the type of recruiter you work with, there are some basic commonalities to their jobs, the most important being that if you impress them, they will often become your advocate.

Corporate Recruiters (also known as Inside Recruiters or Talent Acquisition Recruiters/Specialists/Business Partners) are employed by an employer to fill their open jobs. Corporate recruiters are tracked on how long it takes them to fill the positions that they are assigned, a metric called "Time-to-Fill". An increasing number of employers also track a metric for the quality of the new employees "Quality-of-Hire" (QoH), where retention, performance, and any job promotion of the employees hired by that recruiter is a reflection on his/her performance.

Inside recruiters do not receive commission for filling positions, it is how their job performance and future promotions are evaluated. If you can impress these recruiters, they often turn into an advocate to get you hired. If the organization is small to mid-sized, recruiters typically handle recruitment for multiple departments and job levels. For larger organizations, the talent acquisition teams are bigger, with individual recruiters specializing in specific departments or job levels. Each internal recruiter manages a workload of open job requisitions ("Reqs") typically ranging from 15 to 40 at any given time, depending on the position type.

Agency Recruiters (also called Outside Recruiters or 3rd Party Recruiters) work for staffing companies or independently as their own staffing firm. Outside recruiters have a direct financial incentive to become advocates for strong candidates. These recruiters are not employees of the company you wish to join, they are vendors of that employer. Most third-party recruiters are paid on a contingency basis, which means that the company does not pay them unless they hire a candidate from that recruiter. Most will not submit candidates to their client companies if they are not a good fit because it will make them look bad. Sending a candidate who is a bad fit to a client leads that company to lose confidence in the recruiter and they will start working with a different vendor. If you can impress an outside recruiter and they see a possible successful placement, then they will absolutely become an advocate for you to be hired. These recruiters work with multiple client companies, typically specializing in a particular recruitment area, such as geography, industry, field of work, or mode of employment (e.g., full-time permanent employment, contract, temporary, freelance, or gig work).

Headhunters (also referred to as Executive Recruiters) work for executive search firms or independently as their own firm. Although many outside recruiters like to refer to themselves as a Headhunter or an Executive Recruiter, these terms actually mean an outside recruiter that specializes in high-level positions, such as Directors, VP, and C-Level jobs. They typically do not use job advertisements to find candidates, instead they network and build long-term relationships. These recruiters are paid by the employer on a retained or a contingent fee basis.

Understanding the incentives that recruiters have will help you take advantage of their assistance. Outside recruiters have multiple client companies they work with so they can introduce you to opportunities at more than one employer. Inside recruiters have a deeper knowledge of the company that they work for, and the personalities of the interviewers and decision makers. One or both will likely be involved in decisions about who gets interviewed, moves forward, and the final deliberations on who should receive the job offer. If impressed by you, recruiters are likely to enter you into the hiring process.

Independent headhunters and agency recruitment businesses sign a contract with an employer to provide qualified, pre-screened job candidates. The terms of these contracts outline the fee that the employer will pay for this service. For most contingent fee contracts, the terms specify that if the employer already has that candidate in their application system, no fee will be owed to the recruiter. Thus, by submitting your resume/application to most of the job market, you limit the number of employers that a recruiter can present you to. As a result, outside recruiters have less of an incentive to work with you if you over-submit your application. Make an outside recruiter part of your plan early in your job search and see if they are able to advocate for you with an employer before applying directly. Not all recruiters are created equal of course, but if you find a good one that you trust and enjoy working with, it will benefit you to build a long-term professional relationship with them.

I once worked with a candidate who was a strong fit for the skills portion of the profile I was seeking. In fact, the candidate was overqualified for the position and what the company was willing to pay, but he still wanted to be interviewed for it. I made a good pitch to the hiring manager, but she felt that it just was not a good fit for what she wanted. Typically, there is a concern that overqualified candidates will leave at the first opportunity they have at a higher-level job somewhere else. After I explained to the candidate that the hiring manager was not interested, he did not want to accept that answer. So, without informing me, he contacted the hiring manager directly. She not only told him the same answer that I had given, but she knew right away how inappropriate his actions were by trying to bypass his recruiter and she told me that now she would never consider him for anything in the future. This candidate was never going to get that job, but because of his hubris, he is not a candidate I will ever introduce to any hiring manager again.

Another time I had a single conversation with a candidate who wasn't one of the strongest in his field, but for the right client I thought that I would introduce him into their hiring process. A few months later this candidate emailed and called me, I was working on something else that didn't apply to his background, so I didn't immediately respond. Later that day I received another email and voicemail, the next day the exact same thing, and it became obvious to me that he was not someone I wanted to introduce to my clients. His overly aggressive approach was unprofessional and quickly convinced me that he would harm my relationship with any client company that I introduced him to. I'll never work with this candidate, and most other recruiters and hiring managers will react the same way. Be mindful of the relationships you have if you find a good recruiter.

Some candidates insist on working only with retained recruiters. They apparently either believe that the highest quality recruiters work only on retainer, or that their career has reached a certain level and retained recruiters provide them with more prestige. I've worked both on retained and contingency searches, and many of the best were on a contingency fee structure. Some were exclusive only to me, but I chose not to charge the client a retainer.

Don't pass up an opportunity because it comes as either retained or contingent; there are good and bad searches in both.

When you look for a recruiter to work with, the most reliable way to find a good one is through a referral from someone who has worked with them before. In the absence of a referral, you'll need to screen recruiters. Important factors to consider are their specialization area, such as industry and geography, their experience level, reputation, professionalism, and most importantly, their relationships with employers. If the client companies that they work with match the types of employers you're seeking, and you have a positive impression of the other areas mentioned, then give that recruiter a try.

Building a relationship with a corporate recruiter may take longer. The difference in their role from that of a headhunter makes them more focused on filling current openings in multiple areas. Therefore, if you do not fit their immediate needs, they may not have much time to build a relationship with you. However, if you are targeting specific employers, investing your time with their recruiters could be extremely advantageous for your job search.

Ultimately, you should prioritize connecting with recruiters whom you trust and who treat you with respect.

Mistakes to avoid with Recruiters and Headhunters.

Not responding to calls or emails from recruiters will be viewed as a red flag by most of them. Being too demanding with unrealistic salary or job expectations will imply that you are the type of candidate who will waste a recruiter's time. Having ineffective communication, not putting in the effort to conduct your own personal research, or dishonesty will likely end your relationship with the recruiter. Being too pushy or not being open to feedback will prevent you from improving in your job search and indicate to the recruiter that his time is better spent elsewhere.

Examples Of Messages

Crafting and sending effective messages during a job hunt is a vital part of what separates candidates who are successful, receiving more interviews and job offers, from those who find themselves stagnant in their search. During my career as a recruiter, I have received countless unsolicited messages from candidates and most of these were substandard. Successful job search messages are simple, concise, respectful, and relevant to the recipient. Quality is more important than quantity when it comes to sending messages. I do however recommend that you focus on creating volume for the first couple of weeks, then refine your messages. This will help you avoid getting stuck in "paralysis by analysis" mode and provide a baseline to make your adjustments from. To assist you in constructing successful messages I'm sharing examples sent to various stakeholders, along with my feedback. The messages are addressed to fictional characters to make them more relatable. These characters include Avery, a recruiter, Taylor, a hiring manager, Alex, a professional contact, Morgan, a former coworker, and Casey, a friend of a friend. Use these messages and my reactions to guide your creation of custom and personalized messages.

Message to a recruiter/headhunter.

Dear Avery,

I hope this email finds you well. My name is [Your Name] and I am currently seeking new opportunities in the [Industry/Field] sector. I came across your profile and was impressed by your experience and success in placing top talent with leading companies. I would love the opportunity to network with you and learn more about the opportunities you have available. I have attached my resume for your review, and I would be happy to discuss my background and career goals further in a call or meeting.

Thank you for considering my request and I look forward to the opportunity to connect.

Best regards,

[Your Name]

My reaction:

The message lacks a value proposition which hurts its impact, but if the candidate works in my area of focus, I likely will review their attached resume. If their profile is a good match for the types of roles my clients hire from me, I'd meet with the candidate. Even though I may be willing to meet them, my initial impression from the message is that they're likely not a top candidate. Addressing a business message with "Dear" will stand out and likely be perceived as odd or unprofessional. I appreciate the candidate's willingness to speak with me, without coming across as entitled to my time.

Good morning Avery,

I am writing to introduce myself and express my interest in connecting with you regarding job opportunities in the [Industry/Field]. I have been following your work for some time now and I am impressed by the quality of candidates you have placed in companies I admire. I am a [Your Title/Position] with [Number of Years] years of experience in [Related Skills/Experience].

I am passionate about staying current with industry trends and continuously expanding my skill set, which I believe will make me a valuable asset to any team. I would be honored to have the chance to network with you and discuss any potential job opportunities you may have available. I have attached my resume, bio, and documentation of my accomplishments for your review, and I am available for a call or meeting at your convenience. Thank you for your time and consideration.

Best regards,

[Your Name]

My reaction:

I am unlikely to sift through all the attachments, but I might give your resume a glance. For your initial messages your goal is to capture their attention, not to send them every document you can. The email itself is a tad too lengthy and includes some superfluous words that come across as flattery or salesy, which hurts the effectiveness of the message. The value proposition doesn't sound unique, if you add an accomplishment and years of experience, it would be more impactful. In short, consider trimming down the email and focusing on highlighting your UVP.

Hi Avery,

Please save my resume for any future [Job Type] positions. See attached.

Much appreciated,

[Your Name]

My reaction:

I would have reservations about opening a resume when I lack any context about their background or potential suitability for the types of roles I recruit for. You could add one line outlining a brief overview of your experience, or your value proposition. This would help to pique my interest and increase the likelihood of me keeping your resume on file.

Hello Avery,

My name is [Your Name}, [Your current tittle]. I was referred to you by [Name of Referrer]. I welcome the opportunity to discuss my qualifications for the [Title of Open Position] you are currently recruiting for.

My background includes leading teams of successful [Industry/Function] My passion is developing and coaching talented teams.

Some of my key attributes:

[Attribute #1]

[Attribute #2]

[Attribute #3]

[Attribute #4]

[Attribute #5]

[Attribute #6]

Thank you in advance for your time and consideration. I am available to discuss my qualifications at your convenience.

Sincerely,

[Your Name]

My reaction:

The opening of this message is quite effective and persuasive, particularly if the person who referred the candidate is someone whose opinion I value. However, the list of attributes needs to create value that is unique to this candidate and relates directly to my client's needs. Keeping your messages concise and to-the-point will increase your chances of standing out and achieving positive results.

Hi Avery,

We had connected a few months ago regarding a job you were recruiting for. At that time, I was not interested but my circumstances have changed, and I am currently entertaining new opportunities. Please see my attached updated resume and let me know if you are working on anything that would be a good fit for me.

Thank you,

[Your Name]

My reaction:

This message is excellent. The candidate thoughtfully referenced their connection to a past search and attached their resume. The message itself is clean and concise, allowing the core information to stand out without any distractions. The message does lack a UVP but Avery apparently had determined they were a fit in the past so would likely be motivated to read their resume. Including a reference to a connection with the recipient, such as a past interaction, will increase the effectiveness of your messages.

Hi Avery,

I hope this email finds you well. My name is [Your Name] and I am currently seeking new opportunities in the [Industry/Field] sector. I bring a unique blend of academic achievement and hands-on experience gained through my current role. My data-driven approach, and innovative problem-solving translated into streamlining the operational processes to achieve a 20% efficiency boost. Here is my profile for your review: LinkedIn .com/profile.

I would love the opportunity to network with you. I'm happy to discuss my background and career goals further in a call or meeting.

Thank you for considering my request and I look forward to the opportunity to connect.

Best regards,

[Your Name]

My reaction:

This is a rewritten version of an earlier message, with the value proposition added. You should see how adding a 2-3 sentence UVP can make your messages more impactful. To be successful, your message doesn't have to convince the recruiter that you're the greatest candidate in the world, it just needs to pique their interest. I would click the link to review this candidate's profile, and if they've created a strong candidate brand, I will interview them.

Message to a hiring manager.

Hello Taylor,

I hope this email finds you well. I came across [Company Name] through my job search and I was impressed by the work you are doing in the [Industry] field. I am a [Job Title] with [Number of Years] of experience and I am eager to learn more about any current or future job openings at [Company Name]. I would be grateful if we could schedule a call to discuss my background and your needs in more detail. Thank you for your time and I look forward to hearing back from you.

Best regards,

[Your Name]

My reaction:

This message is not very impactful. Perhaps if the candidate's job title and years of experience closely aligns with a current opening with that hiring manager, they might respond. Although the candidate does attempt to provide a reason for wanting to speak with the hiring manager, it isn't compelling enough. Not including your value proposition, attaching your resume, or providing a link to your profile in your messages makes it difficult for hiring managers to evaluate whether responding is worth their time.

Hi Taylor,

I hope this email finds you well. I came across [Company Name] through my job search and I was impressed by the opportunities that you are offering in the [Industry] field. I am a [Job Title] with [Number of Years] of experience and I believe that I would be a great fit for one of your current or future job openings. I would be grateful if we could schedule a call to discuss my background and your needs in more detail. Thank you for your time and I look forward to connecting with you soon.

Best regards,

[Your Name]

My reaction:

While this email message starts off well with personalized language addressed to the hiring manager's company, it begins to falter towards the end. Rather than conveying a specific fit for a particular job opening or a value proposition, it becomes vague. This makes the message feel like spam, which weakens the rest of the message.

It's important for you to use your UVP to clearly and concisely demonstrate that you're a fit for the company's needs. If there is a current opening that you are targeting, briefly explain your interest and how you are a fit. Without at least an attached resume or link to your profile, your messages will have low rates of success. This message lacks a compelling reason for the hiring manager to take the time to speak to respond.

Good afternoon Taylor,

I hope this email finds you well. I am writing to you today because I am very interested in learning more about the

[Currently Posted Job] opportunity that you are responsible for at [Company Name]. I am a [Job Title] with [Number of Years] of experience in [Industry].

I would appreciate any direction you can provide on how I can be considered for this opening as I know it is a good fit for my background.

Thank you for your time and I look forward to connecting with you soon.

Best regards,

[Your Name]

My reaction:

The message lacks a value proposition but is still effective. It is concise, clear, and provides basic information about experience so Taylor can evaluate a potential fit for the open position. The email is specifically tailored for the job opening. Even without a UVP, an attached resume or link to profile, Taylor can quickly evaluate whether to forward this email to the Talent Acquisition department or respond directly to the candidate. This message demonstrates how effective and impactful a concise and targeted approach can be in making a strong first impression.

Hi Taylor,

I am writing to you today because I am very interested in learning more about the [Currently Posted Job] opportunity that you are responsible for at [Company Name]. In my sales role at [Previous Company], I consistently outperformed targets by 20%, strategically securing key accounts and boosting revenue by 30% within the first year alone. Here is a link to my updated profile: LinkedIn .com/profile.

I would appreciate any direction you can provide on how I can be considered for this opening as I know it is a good fit for my background.

Thank you for your time and I look forward to connecting with you soon.

Best regards,

[Your Name]

My reaction:

This is the same message as the last email, but with a UVP. It is still concise, clear, and is now an even more compelling message which will stand out to Taylor more than the previous email. This version also includes a link to an updated profile. If the candidate aligned their profile with their unique value proposition and candidate brand, this email will be very persuasive and make a strong first impression.

Message to a professional contact.

Hello Alex,

I hope this email finds you well. I was recently impressed by your [achievement/professional background/etc.] and I was hoping to tap into your professional network for my job search. I am currently seeking new opportunities in the [Industry] field and I would be grateful if you could introduce me to one of your contacts who may be able to provide me with some insight or guidance. I am eager to learn more about the industry and I believe that connecting with one of your contacts would be an excellent first step.

Thank you for your time and I look forward to hearing back from you.

Best regards,

[Your Name]

My reaction:

This message provides a clear reason for the introduction, but it would have been helpful to provide some more details about their experience and skills. With a value proposition or link to profile, this type of email would be more impactful. It is also more persuasive to specify which contact you'd like to be introduced to.

Dear Alex,

I hope this email finds you in good spirits. I am writing to you today to ask for your help in my job search. I am a [Job Title] with [Number of Years] of experience and I am interested in exploring new opportunities in the [Industry] field. I was impressed by your professional network, and I was hoping that you could introduce me to one of your contacts who may be able to provide me with some insight or guidance on the job market in this field. I would be honored to connect with one of your contacts and learn more about the industry.

Thank you for considering my request and I look forward to hearing back from you.

Best regards,

[Your Name]

My reaction:

The message is simple and clear, but generic and not persuasive. By not mentioning a specific contact that they are interested in meeting, the message seems impersonal and spammy. The job seeker is also requesting a favor without offering anything in return. It's important for you to offer something of value to the people you reach out to such as reciprocating introductions for Alex with your network contacts. This message comes across as the exact message that the job seeker is sending to a hundred other people.

Hi Alex,

I hope this email finds you well. We've been connected online for some time now and I have been impressed by your professional background and achievements in the [Industry] field. I am currently seeking new opportunities in this area, and I would be grateful if you could introduce me to any of your contacts who may be able to help me grow my local network. I am seeking a role as a [target job] and bring [years of experience] years of successful experience with me.

Thank you for considering my request and I truly would appreciate any assistance that you can provide.

Best regards,

[Your Name]

My reaction:

This message would benefit from some tweaks to make it more impactful. Specifically, the job seeker should consider suggesting a specific contact or asking Alex for recommendations of which contacts would be most helpful. Asking for Alex's opinion would make the request more actionable. Adding a statement about returning the favor in the future can help to build a stronger relationship and increase the chances of Alex being willing to assist. Overall, the message is polite and professional, but there are small adjustments that could make it even more effective.

Hi Alex,

I hope you are doing well. We've been connected online for some time now and I have been impressed by your professional background and achievements in the [Industry] field. As an experienced nurse myself with a background in critical care at [Previous Hospital], I've successfully reduced patient readmission rates by 30% through personalized care plans. I have a commitment to excellence and am currently seeking new job opportunities. I would be grateful if you could recommend the best people in your local network for me to speak with, even better if you can make the introduction. Of course, I'd be happy to return the favor anytime you need it.

Thank you for considering my request and I truly would appreciate any assistance that you can provide.

Best regards,

[Your Name]

My reaction:

This is the same message as the one before, but with a UVP, a request for recommendations, and an offer to reciprocate the favor. Hopefully you can see how a few small changes can increase the impact of your messages and your odds of success.

Message to a former coworker.

Hello Morgan,

I hope this email finds you well. It has been great catching up with you after all these years. I am writing to you today to ask for your help in my job search. I am currently seeking new opportunities in the [Industry] field and I was hoping that you could introduce me to one of your contacts who may be able to provide me with some insight or guidance. Your professional network is highly regarded, and I believe that connecting with one of your contacts would be an excellent first step.

Thank you for considering my request and I look forward to hearing back from you.

Best regards,

[Your Name]

My reaction:

This message would benefit from a more personal touch. While it does establish the connection between the job seeker and Morgan, it feels a bit impersonal and generic at the end. The message does a good job of reminding Morgan of their recent interaction and making a request. But to make it more effective, you should specify which contact/contacts you'd like Morgan to introduce you to and make the message more concise. Since the job seeker and Morgan worked together, the message doesn't need to include a value proposition, link to profile, or resume but if they haven't worked together in several years or didn't work directly with one another, I would recommend including them.

Dear Morgan,

I hope this email finds you in good spirits. I was recently reminded of our time working together at [Company Name] and I want to reach out to you for help in my job search. I am currently seeking new opportunities in the [Industry] field and I was hoping that you could introduce me to one of your contacts who might be able to provide me with some insight or guidance. I believe that connecting with one of your contacts would be an excellent first step for my job search.

Thank you for your time and I look forward to hearing back from you.

Best regards,

[Your Name]

My reaction:

This message to a former co-worker is effective. It provides a personal touch by connecting with Morgan through their shared experience, although being more specific on which contacts, they wish to be introduced to would be more impactful. It's always a good idea for you to offer future assistance in return. Overall, a few more tweaks and this message will yield more positive results.

Hi Morgan,

I hope that you're still doing well since we saw each other last. For the past couple of years since we worked together at [Company Name] I have been adding to my experience as a [Job Title]. I am now beginning a new job search, and I'm hoping that you can introduce me to one or more of your contacts. As I remember you are well connected, and I would appreciate any help that you can provide as I search for my next opportunity. As always, feel free to reach out to me if you have any questions or you would just like to catch up.

Thank you,

[Your Name]

My reaction:

This message to a former coworker is concise and effective. It establishes a personal connection and shares a common memory, then clearly explains the job search, and makes a specific request. The message does miss an opportunity to offer to return the favor in the future, which would strengthen the relationship. Nonetheless, this message is likely to have a positive response. Because it refers to additional experience since working together, you should add your UVP.

Hi Morgan,

I hope that you're still doing well since we saw each other last. For the past couple of years since we worked together at [Company Name] I have been adding to my experience as a financial analyst. With my work at [Previous Company], I orchestrated a streamlined budgeting process that resulted in a 20% cost reduction.

I am now beginning a new job search, and I'm hoping that you can introduce me to one or more of your contacts. As I remember you are well connected so I trust your judgement on who would be the best person for me to connect with, and I would appreciate any introductions that you can provide. As always, feel free to reach out to me if I can return the favor in any way, you have any questions, or would just like to catch up.

Thank you,

[Your Name]

My reaction:

This is the same as the last message, with a few notable tweaks. It now includes a value proposition, implies Morgan should recommend the best contacts, and offers to return the favor. The message is still concise, but hopefully you can see that it will likely have more impact when Morgan reads it compared to the previous email.

Hello Morgan,

I am currently seeking a new opportunity. Please let me know if you hear of any leads, and which of your contacts would be best for me to network with about my job search.

I appreciate your help and as always, I'm happy to return the favor.

Best regards,

[Your Name]

My reaction:

This message should only be sent to a contact or former co-worker who you have a good relationship with, and that is already familiar with your value proposition.

Message to a friend of a friend.

Hello Casey,

I hope this email finds you well. My name is [Your Name] and I am a friend of [Your Friend's Name]. They recently mentioned that you work in the [Industry] field and I was hoping to network with you about potential job opportunities. I am currently seeking a new role and I would love to hear about your experience in the industry and any advice or guidance you could offer.

Thank you for your time and I look forward to connecting with you.

Best regards,

[Your Name]

My reaction:

This message is good, but the request for help is too vague. You could suggest meeting for coffee or lunch to establish a one-on-one connection. After a direct connection has been established, then you can request to be introduced to one of Casey's connections or ask for other assistance. The message does a good job of establishing the connection to Casey, and that the writer is in a job search. It's clear and concise but could be even more impactful with a couple of changes.

Dear Casey,

I hope this email finds you well. My name is [Your Name] and I was referred to you by [Your Friend's Name]. They mentioned that you have extensive experience in the [Industry] field and I was hoping to network with you about potential job opportunities. I am currently seeking new opportunities and I would appreciate the chance to hear about your experience and any advice you may have to offer.

Thank you for your time and I look forward to connecting with you.

Best regards,

[Your Name]

My reaction:

The job seeker starts off well by establishing the connection. However, it becomes generic and fails to ask or suggest a way to meet in person. Offering to buy Casey lunch or coffee in exchange for their time and insights could make the message more effective. Including an offer to reciprocate the favor might make networking more appealing. If you use a message like this to make a personal connection, then it can lead to asking for introductions or other assistance in the future.

Dear Casey,

I hope this email finds you well. My name is [Your Name] and I was referred to you by [Your Friend's Name]. They mentioned that you work in the [Industry] field and I'd like to network with you as part of my current job search. I'm a physical therapist with a track record of facilitating accelerated recovery for post-operative patients at [Previous Clinic], achieving a 25% reduction in rehabilitation time. I am currently seeking new opportunities and I would appreciate the chance to meet with you for lunch and hear about your experience and any advice you may have to offer. In return, I am happy to help you in any way I can in the future.

Thank you for your time and I look forward to connecting with you.

Best regards,

[Your Name]

My reaction:

This is the same as the previous message, but with a UVP, a direct request to meet for lunch, and an offer to reciprocate. By making just these small tweaks to the original message, you can increase the chances of the message yielding positive results. Step one is for you to meet and make a genuine connection with Casey, step two will be to ask for introductions, referrals, or insights on the current job market.

Thank you emails/cards after networking.

Hi [Name],

I want to thank you for taking the time to speak with me at the [event name] last week. Your insights and guidance regarding [topic discussed] were incredibly valuable to me, and I appreciate your willingness to share your expertise.

It was a pleasure to connect with someone who shares my passion for [relevant industry or field], and I am excited about the potential opportunities that may arise from our conversation. I look forward to staying in touch and continuing our dialogue about [related topics].

Again, thank you for your time and expertise. I hope to have the opportunity to connect with you again soon.

Best regards,

[Your Name]

My reaction:

This message needs to be more concise but is effective for building a long-term networking relationship. It would be beneficial to remind the recipient of one or two impressive things about your profile that may have stood out to them during the conversation. This would help to reinforce your personal candidate brand and leave a lasting impression. Removing some of the generic language will help with the length and impact of this message.

Hello [Name],

I just want to thank you for taking the time to speak with me at [event/location]. Your insights into the industry and your personal experiences were great for me to hear. I appreciate the opportunity to learn from you and gain a better understanding of the industry.

Your willingness to share your knowledge and expertise has given me a lot to think about as I continue my job search. I am grateful for the connection we have made.

Please don't hesitate to reach out if there is anything I can do to reciprocate your generosity or if there are any ways that I can be of assistance to you in the future. Thank you again for your time and consideration.

Best regards,

[Your Name]

My reaction:

This message builds towards a long-term professional relationship that could lead to many benefits for your job search. It is notable how it does not make the connection feel one-sided and instead expresses gratitude and offers reciprocated assistance. This type of approach makes a positive impression on the reader and encourages them to make an extra effort to help you. Overall, this message is a great example of networking in a way that is both respectful and mutually beneficial.

Hello [Name],

Thank you for taking the time to speak with me at the event yesterday. I appreciated your insights on the industry and your suggestions on how to enhance my skills. I'm particularly excited about your recent project in [specific area related to job] and would love to learn more about it.

After speaking with you, I am even more confident that my [specific skill or strength] would make me an asset to your team. I look forward to the opportunity to discuss how I can contribute to your organization in the future. Thank you again for your time and advice.

Best regards,

[Your Name]

My reaction:

The job seeker does a good job of reminding the hiring manager of their previous interaction and making a connection to their needs, but the ask is not specific enough. Requesting a meeting within a certain timeframe would make it more likely for the hiring manager to respond. You want to remind the hiring manager of your candidate brand, so you should add one or two impressive things about your profile that may have stood out to them during your conversation. Your message should also be personalized to make it less like a form letter.

Hi [Name],

Thank you for taking the time to speak with me at the event yesterday. I appreciated your insights on the airline industry and your suggestions on how to enhance my skills. I'm particularly excited about your recent expansion project in adding global service routes and would love to learn more about it.

As a reminder, my track record as a flight attendant includes fostering a 25% increase in passenger satisfaction ratings through personalized attention.

After speaking with you, I am even more confident that my unique blend of hospitality and safety expertise would make me an asset to your team. I look forward to discussing more about how I can contribute to your airline. Thank you again for your time and advice.

Best regards,

[Your Name]

My reaction:

This is the previous message, but with a personal candidate brand and a more personalized tone. Again, small tweaks to your messages can yield much better results. You should reassess your messages every so often throughout your job search.

Thank you emails/cards after an interview.

Hi [Interviewer],

Thank you for the opportunity to interview for the [Position] role. I appreciate the time you took to discuss the position with me and to learn more about my experience. Our discussion about my [positive point 1] and [positive point 2] reinforced my confidence that I am a fit for the position. I do want to reassure you that [potential negative] will have no bearing on the value that I will bring to the team. Thank you again for your time and I look forward to hearing back from you.

Best regards,

[Your Name]

My reaction:

This is an excellent example of how to write a concise, impactful thank you message after an interview. It's important to highlight one or two positive points that came out during the interview to remind them why you're a strong candidate. If any concerns were raised during the interview, you should address them briefly to mitigate any doubts the interviewer might have. This approach can greatly increase your chances of moving forward in the hiring process.

Hello [Interviewer's Name],

Thank you for taking the time to interview me for the [Position] role at [Company Name]. I appreciate the opportunity to learn more about the company and the position.

During the interview, I was impressed by the company's dedication to [something specific discussed in the interview]. I am confident that my experience and skills in [skill or strength discussed in the interview] make me a strong match for the role.

Thank you again for considering me for the position, and I look forward to hearing from you soon.

Best regards,

[Your Name]

My reaction:

This thank you message is effective and hits all the right notes. It is brief and to the point, yet still manages to convey the job seeker's appreciation for the interview and interest in the position. It is crucial to remind the interviewer of your personal candidate brand and highlight positives from the interview, as it can help stand out from the candidates you're competing against.

"Thank you for taking the time to interview me. I appreciated the opportunity to discuss my background and learn more about the company. I was especially excited about the prospect of working with such a dynamic team and the potential to contribute to the company's growth. I recognize that my lack of experience in [a specific area] might be a concern, but I am willing to put in the extra effort to bring myself up to speed quickly and bring value to the team."

My reaction:

This is a very casual message that does not include a salutation. While this type of message might be effective in an industry with casual company cultures, it will not be successful in a highly professional field. It does cover the essential points, but it would benefit from including a positive reminder of the job seeker's background that was discussed during the interview.

You can learn more about thank you notes and the entire interview process by searching for "SoaringME" to find our ultimate guides on successful interviewing for various jobs.

The above messages should be modified to your style, and you can always create your own. Keep in mind that brevity, relevance, being respectful, professional, including your unique value proposition, and candidate brand are all keys to creating impactful messages that yield results. It's important to include enough information so that the recipient can understand your profile and what you're requesting. Most importantly, you need to have proactively sent messages as part of your comprehensive job search plan.

For any initial message that you don't receive a response to, you should follow up once within two weeks. Your follow up message should reference your initial attempt and reiterate your same points using different verbiage. Remain polite, respectful, relevant, and unentitled in your approach. If you still do not receive a response, you might send one more follow up message after at least one month.

Mistakes that you need to avoid.

Writing generic and impersonal messages tops the list of common mistakes you should avoid. Overly lengthy, or unfocused messages quickly lose the reader's attention. Failing to tailor messages to specific opportunities and individuals will make your message blend into the background. An overly casual tone, grammatical errors and spelling mistakes will be perceived as unprofessional. Irrelevant or overly frequent messages will come across as spam. Being overly aggressive or pushy in communication, not following up on your previous interactions, and expecting immediate replies give the impression that you are not someone worth networking with. The exception to this is the rare occasions when the desired candidate profile includes those aggressive attributes.

Traditional Search Methods

Job boards, social media, job fairs, and soft recruiting events are a part of any successful job search plan. Including these tools as part of your overall comprehensive plan will help you reach your goals. The key is to not rely exclusively on these tools to find your next job. You need to take a more holistic approach, but let's review these more traditional methods.

Job Boards.

Every job seeker is likely aware of job boards, this is typically where most job applications come from. Not all job boards are created equal, and some may have more postings in your desired field or location than others. It's essential that you research job boards thoroughly to determine which ones will be most useful specifically for your job search.

It's also important to keep track of which jobs you have applied for, including the date, job description and any other relevant details. Failing to keep track of these details will result in not remembering the profile and how you fit that specific job when they call you for an interview.

As I mentioned earlier when speaking about networking, one of the most effective techniques that I have seen candidates use is to follow up their job application with a message to one of their contacts. Reaching out to an employee or mutual connection with the recruiter can create a "pull-through" effect for your application. Simply notifying your connection that you have applied to the company and asking them to message the recruiter will greatly increase the odds that you receive an interview.

Finally, if you post your resume on a job board, make sure to refresh it every few weeks to keep it up to date and relevant. This keeps you visible to recruiters who routinely search for the newest resumes on a site, increasing your chances of being contacted for a job opportunity.

Social Media.

Searching for job openings using social media platforms is often overlooked. Some platforms such as LinkedIn, X/Twitter, and even Facebook try to be both social media and a job board, with posted jobs as part of their site. Some hiring managers and recruiters post about job openings in their feed that might not be listed in job advertisements. You should search social media posts for those that mention jobs you are seeking, as this can provide you with leads that other candidates have missed.

LinkedIn has features such as listing yourself as "Open to Work" or "Open to Networking", both of which can help attract the attention of recruiters and benefit your search. This is true for most but not all recruiters. As a headhunter I pay very little attention to these features as I focus on the skills and experience and reach out to candidates who fit the profile I seek, even if they aren't listed as actively looking for their next job.

Posting on social media yourself and announcing that you are "open" or "looking" for your next career opportunity can be very effective. These types of posts make your profile more noticeable, engage with contacts in your network who might refer you for a role they're aware of, and they help recruiters find you when they search social media. The most effective posts will include your value proposition and a concise description of the type of opportunity you're seeking.

Examples of effective posts announcing your job search.

"I'm looking to bring my 5+ years of excellent customer service representative experience to my next healthcare career opportunity. Please share my background with your professional network."

"Job search!

If you're looking for someone to build out an XYZ based platform, let me know!"

"After nearly 10 incredible years with XYZ Corporation, marked by many milestones, I find myself poised for the next step in my career journey. Despite our record-breaking quarter, XYZ has announced a reduction in the workforce. I am open to my next

Brand Manager opportunity, please let me know about any job leads in the field."

Job Fairs.

Attending a job fair, whether it's online or in-person, requires a strategic approach to make the most of your limited time with hiring managers and recruiters. Preparation is key to creating a positive first impression, and this includes dressing appropriately for the job and perfecting your elevator pitch. Doing thorough research on the employers beforehand can help you ask relevant questions that will make you stand out among other candidates.

In a crowded job fair, recruiters and hiring managers are exposed to dozens, if not hundreds, of job seekers each day. To make a memorable impression, you need to be prepared, engaged, and professional. Dressing the part is important as it contributes to the impression you leave on the hiring managers and recruiters. You should be prepared with your elevator pitch and UVP to quickly communicate your value to potential employers and stand out from other job seekers. In a virtual setting, test your equipment to make sure that your technology is functioning beforehand to avoid technical difficulties.

Following up after a job fair shows employers that you are serious about the job and demonstrates your professionalism. Sending a thank-you note or email to recruiters and hiring managers can have a big impact on the success of your job search.

Soft Recruiting Events.

Soft recruiting, also known as passive recruiting, is a popular approach in some industries that involves attending recruitment networking or social events. These events can be on-site at an employer's place of business, or off-site and might be sponsored by a single employer, an association, or a recruiting agency. To make the most of these events, it's important to prepare and approach them strategically.

Researching the company/companies that you plan to target is important to help you make a good impression. Explaining why you're interested in a specific employer and how you can add value to them allows you to stand out from the crowd. Try to understand their needs and determine the value that you can offer. Having a strong social media presence that reflects your personal candidate brand will strengthen the positive impression that you demonstrate.

You should dress appropriately for whatever the event is. This means showing respect for the dress code and presenting yourself in a professional, polished manner. Being prepared with your elevator pitch and value proposition is also key to differentiating yourself from other candidates.

You should speak with as many recruiters and hiring managers as possible in a natural and authentic manner. Networking with other candidates at the event can be an excellent way to exchange information and learn about other job openings.

Ask questions about the work environment and company culture as this information can provide you with valuable insights into the company's needs and help you tailor your approach. Like all your networking efforts, you need to follow up after the event. Send a thank-you note, or email while your profile is fresh in their minds.

Mistakes to avoid with traditional job search methods.

Over-reliance on job boards and failure to explore other avenues, such as networking or reaching out to recruiters is the biggest mistake that job seekers make. It will limit the potential opportunities you have and prevent you from standing out among the large number of candidates that are seeking the same jobs. Indiscriminately applying to every job advertisement, regardless of your qualifications or interest, leads to wasted time, limits the ability of outside recruiters to assist you, and hurts your candidate brand which lowers the effectiveness of your other efforts. Neglecting to tailor your resumes and cover letters decreases the chances of obtaining an interview. Being unprepared to talk about your qualifications, and not following up after the event will result in missing out on job opportunities.

Comprehensive Job Search Plan

Understanding the components of a successful job search is not enough, you need to put those techniques and methods together into a comprehensive strategic plan. How formal a plan needs to be will vary, but having a well thought out strategy will increase your likelihood of success and help you avoid common mistakes. The more competitive the job market you're searching in, the more time you need to spend on creating a roadmap. Making your plan more concrete will help you keep yourself accountable for completing the activities that lead to success. As Benjamin Franklin once said, "By failing to prepare, you are preparing to fail.".

If you are in a field with a low unemployment rate, then you likely can find a job without a detailed roadmap. However, if you want the most desirable positions in your field, making a strong plan will expand the possibilities available to you.

In 2018 there were a couple of interesting developments with regards to employment and job searching. For the first time in over 20 years, there were more job openings than people to fill them. That same year, the US Bureau of Labor Statistics gathered job search data with a supplement to their Current Population Survey (CPS). From this data we learned that it took jobseekers on average six applications to obtain one interview, but this is likely different in a market when there are more job seekers than openings. The positions with hundreds of applications will likely have less than one out of six receive an interview, and the positions with ten applications could have interviews with half of the applicants. The one out of every six, or about 17% of your applications is a good benchmark for you to start with in your job search plan. Using the methods and techniques in this book should improve your ratio of interviews, but you will certainly need to target multiple jobs to reach your goals.

Taking the ideal profile and employer sources of candidates into consideration should play a crucial role in formulating your strategy. Use the following as your guide as you map out your job search plan and goals.

Steps to formulating a successful job search plan.

1. Spell out your career goals.

2. Research potential employers.

3. Learn the ideal candidate profile.

4. Conduct an honest self-assessment.

5. Develop your Unique Value Proposition (UVP).

6. Create your candidate brand.

7. Formulate your elevator pitch.

8. Update your resume and cover letter.

9. Optimize your online profiles.

10. Create your networking target list.

11. Set clear and measurable goals.

12. Network.

13. Work with recruiters and headhunters.

14. Tap into the hidden job market.

15. Identify job targets.

16. Participate in career fairs and soft recruiting events.

17. Apply for jobs.

18. Prepare for interviews.

19. Follow up after networking and interviewing.

20. Reassess and improve your job search plan as you go.

21. Be patient and focus only on the things that you have control over.

Setting your goals.

Naturally the end goal of your job search is to land a job that you want. To get there you will need to plan a successful process, and setting measurable goals is a critical part of making your search work. Your goals should be broken down into two main time categories: before and after your job search outreach. All these goals need to be specific, measurable, achievable, relevant, and time-bound (SMART). Before addressing your outreach activities, start basic with goals about which day you need to complete items 1-10 on the list of steps I just covered (UVP, personal candidate brand, optimize social media, update resume, and cover letter, formulate elevator pitch, and create networking target list). I would also include doing an evaluation of available job search tools (next chapter) in your first group of goals. Measure your outreach activities by tracking the items 12-19 on the list of steps (number of messages you send, meetings with recruiters, face-to-face events attended, online events, applications submitted, follow up messages sent, number of interviews - it's a good idea to break interviews down into phone, first round, second round interviews, etc.).

When managing recruiters, I track their activities based on the idea that the interview process is like a funnel. At the top of this funnel there are usually a large number of initial applicants and as we progress through the process, the pool of candidates gets progressively smaller. I then calculate the ratios of how many candidates it takes at each stage in the process for a recruiter to end up with a successful hire at the end. These ratios help me identify any points in the process that the recruiter needs extra coaching on. If any of the conversion ratio shows that they are having trouble moving candidates at a certain stage, then I know where they need improvement. The best way to set your activity goals is to track how many applications it takes to obtain an interview, how many messages to get a response, how many of those result in a meeting, and so on. If your ratios show that you have any points with low conversion rates in your search process, then that is where you need to adjust.

Regularly reassess and refine your goals based on feedback, market trends, or changes in your career priorities. Again, you need to maintain a positive mindset and have perseverance throughout your job search, recognizing that setbacks are a natural part of reaching your goals.

Job Search Tools

In the past the most organized job seekers would use a spreadsheet to keep track of where and for what they had applied. Some would email themselves the job advertisement and the version of their resume and cover letter that they used. When an employer called them, they knew the details of the job and their application. Today, there are tools that will make these and other tasks easier and more efficient. You will be much more effective if you use some type of system that you are comfortable with to organize your search.

I'm listing some job search tools that are available at the time of writing this book. Technology and especially the AI-powered tools are changing and evolving rapidly so in addition to these listed tools, you should also do a search for AI powered services that help job seekers to explore what else might be available.

Creating your job search plan.

- JibberJobber.
- Careerflow.ai.
- Huntr.
- Trello.
- Notion.

Crafting your candidate brand and elevator pitch.

- BrandYourself.
- Rezi.

Creating your resume and cover letter.

- Resume.io.
- Zety.
- Rezi.
- TopCV.
- Jobscan.
- VisualCV.
- VMock.
- VelvetJobs.
- ChatGPT.

Searching and mass applying for jobs.

- Simplify.jobs.
- Autoapply.io.
- Aiapply.co.
- Bulkapply.ai.
- Jobwizard.newpage.im.
- Lazyapply.
- Tealhq.
- Livecareer.
- Sonara.ai.
- Massive.

Finding recruiters and headhunters.

- Oya's Directory of Recruiters on i-Recruit.
- Experteer.
- Headhunters Directory.
- Glassdoor.
- Indeed.
- LinkedIn.

Social media platforms to consider.

- LinkedIn.
- "X" fka Twitter.
- Facebook.
- Jobcase.
- Meetup.
- RippleMatch.
- Viadeo.
- Experteer.
- Xing.

Communication tools to consider.

- Slack.
- Discord.
- Microsoft Teams.
- WhatsApp.
- Skype.
- Telegram.
- WeChat.
- LINE.

Locating job fairs for your search.

- Eventbrite.

- NationalCareerFairs.

- CareerFairPlus.

- JobFairsIn.

- JobFairsNearMe.

- Jobcase.

- CareerOneStop.

- Indeed.

- Glassdoor.

- LinkedIn.

- SimplyHired.

Reference guides for salary information.

- Comprehensive.io.

- Glassdoor.

- Salary.com.

- PayScale.

- Indeed Salary.

- Comparably.

If you have found value in this book, please take a moment to leave a rating and inform others.

Visit SoaringME.com or ask your favorite bookstore for our other books to help your career.

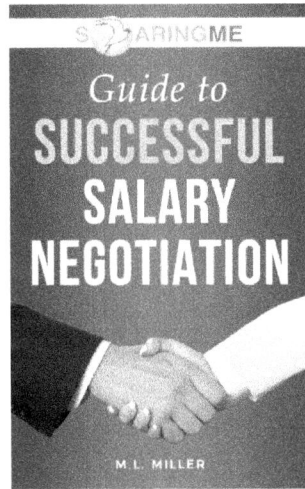

We also have several Ultimate Guides to Job Interviewing for specific careers.

About the Author

M.L. Miller was born in Goldendale, Washington, raised in Oregon, and has since lived in various locations across America. Currently, he and his wife Wilawan divide their time between the United States and Thailand.

Having studied Economics/Finance at the University of Hartford in Connecticut, M.L. began a career in recruitment in

1997, working for hundreds of client companies from Fortune 100 large corporations to start-ups. During this time, he has conducted somewhere between twenty and thirty thousand job interviews and has hired thousands of employees in a variety of roles from entry-level to C-Suite and Board-Level. During his career he managed a corporate recruiting team, increasing their hires by over thirty-three percent in under two years. He started Ethical Recruiters, Inc., an executive recruitment firm and later SoaringME, a company that educates candidates on how to be more successful in job interviewing.

Within this framework, M.L. has also published several books related to the subject:

SoaringME The Ultimate Guide to Successful Job Searching.

SoaringME The Ultimate Guide to Successful Job Interviewing.

SoaringME COMPANION WORKBOOK The Ultimate Guide to Successful Job Interviewing.

SoaringME.com: Guide to Successful Salary Negotiation.

He also has several Ultimate Guides on interviewing for specific careers.

In his free time, M.L. is an avid cyclist and has ridden the annual 200-mile Seattle-to-Portland bike ride five times so far. He also enjoys traveling domestically and internationally.

M.L. has worked with homeless military veterans for a couple of years through a non-profit organization. He used his experience to help them improve interviewing skills, write resumes, and obtain employment to get back on their feet. He also raises money for children's mental health charities.

In the future, M.L. plans to continue his career in talent acquisition. His personal goal is to one day combine his love of cycling and travel to complete 100-mile bike rides on five different continents.

His favorite quote is "Every strike brings me closer to the next home run." – Babe Ruth.

www.ingramcontent.com/pod-product-compliance
Lightning Source LLC
Chambersburg PA
CBHW071425210326
41597CB00020B/3660